Old Rosehearty, Sandhaven and New

Douglas G. Lockhart

ROSEHEARTY.

Text © Douglas G. Lockhart, 2013
First published in the United Kingdom, 2013,
by Stenlake Publishing Ltd.
Telephone: 01290 551122
www.stenlake.co.uk

Printed by
Berforts, 17 Burgess Road, Hastings, TN35 4NR

ISBN 9781840336269

**The publishers regret that they cannot supply
copies of any pictures featured in this book**

Further Reading

The websites and books listed below were used by the author during his research. None of them is available from Stenlake Publishing. Those interested in finding out more are advised to contact their local bookshop or reference library.

Anson, P. F., *Fishing Boats and Fisher Folk on the East Coast of Scotland*, J. M. Dent & Sons Ltd, London, 1930.
Cramond, W., *The Church of Aberdour*, Fraserburgh Advertiser, n.d. [1896].
Hamilton, H. (ed.), *The County of Aberdeen, The Third Statistical Account*, Vol. 7, Collins, Glasgow, 1960.
McKean, C., *Banff & Buchan: An Illustrated Architectural Guide*, RIAS, Edinburgh, 1990.
McLeman, J. M., *Rosehearty As It Was*, Rosehearty, n.d.
Pratt, J. B., *Buchan*, Blackwood and Sons, Edinburgh, 1858.
Randall, David J. (ed.), *The Kirks of Buchan Presbytery*, W. Peters and Son, Turriff, 2000.
Smith, A., *A New History of Aberdeenshire*, L. Smith, Aberdeen, 1875.
Taylor, J., *Rosehearty: Its History as a Fishing Town*, Rosehearty Heritage Society, 1982.

The New Statistical Account of Scotland, Vol. 12: Aberdeen (1845): www.electricscotland.com/history/statistical/volume12.htm
Ordnance Survey maps provided by the National Library of Scotland: www.maps.nls.uk/os/index.html

Acknowledgements

I would like to thank the staffs of Aberdeen Central Library, Aberdeenshire Library HQ, Oldmeldrum, Aberdeenshire Archives, Old Aberdeen, National Records of Scotland, Edinburgh and National Library of Scotland, Edinburgh for their help with my enquiries. I am grateful to William Crawford, Dorothy Dewar, Geoff Marston, Eric Simpson, Katharine Stout and June Whyte for the information they provided. Lastly, several collections of estate management papers that are in private ownership have been consulted and I wish to acknowledge the assistance of Andrew Dingwall Fordyce of Brucklay and the late George Watson of Middlemuir.

Introduction

The three places featured in this book can be found on the north coast of Aberdeenshire, a few miles west of Fraserburgh. Rosehearty has the largest population and has a fascinating variety of streets, housing and churches as well as two harbours. Sandhaven with its older neighbour Pitullie are smaller, though like Rosehearty both have had a strong commitment to fishing. New Aberdour was founded as a planned village at the end of the eighteenth century. The cliffs and rocky coastline, scene of many shipwrecks, and the rural hinterland where churches, schools and small shops once served farming communities also feature among the photographs.

Today, Rosehearty has a population of almost 1,200, a little down from the peak of 1,400 reached at the height of the herring fishing boom in the early 1880s. The origins of the burgh can be traced back to 1681 when King Charles II granted Lord Pitsligo a charter, though a small settlement of fishermen already lived in the area. Fifteen years later twenty-five seamen, many of whom would have been fishermen, were recorded in the Poll Tax returns. The town took shape in the area around the Square and along the seafront in Link Street (later Union Street). A separate seatown evolved to the north-west near the west pier (later North Street). The nineteenth century saw the development of the new town with its distinctive grid of streets sandwiched between the Square and the seatown. Rosehearty grew rapidly in this period as it was able to harness many of the benefits from its involvement with fishing and coastal shipping. Harbour facilities were expanded in the 1860s with the construction of a new pier at Port Rae. Other businesses flourished, particularly shops and inns, and a branch of the Union Bank opened.

The concentration of fishing activity at the larger ports had an adverse impact on smaller fishing settlements which had tidal harbours. After the First World War, Rosehearty tried to diversify into the holiday trade. There was already a golf course on the links, and tennis courts and a bowling green were opened. Hotels ran advertising campaigns to attract visitors and the town council promoted an annual gala week. In 1959, a sea water swimming pool was built in the harbour, but its short season of little more than three months demonstrates how difficult it was for the town to diversify into tourism.

The town council was also active in improving housing conditions. The replacement of substandard properties occurred in Pitsligo Street and Union Street while a scheme on the outskirts gradually took shape between the late 1930s and late 1960s. Some familiar features have inevitably been lost. For example, the post office in the Square is now a hotel, the Victorian school has been replaced by a large new educational complex, and the construction of a function suite at the Forbes Arms Hotel at a stroke rendered its appearance unrecognisable. However, many of the scenes in the photographs can still be viewed today, moreover traditional events such as bonfire night and the annual Mason's Walk continue to be enthusiastically supported. Rosehearty certainly deserves its accolade as an historic town.

Pitullie is a typical example of a seatown where houses are arranged gable end to the sea and each property is close to its neighbour and separated by a narrow strip of grass or gravel. The growth of herring fishing and coastal trade in the nineteenth century ushered in a wave of investment in new harbours and such developments were often accompanied by planned villages. This explains the founding of Sandhaven near Pitullie in the late 1830s. New harbours were built throughout the Moray Firth area, but unfortunately many proved too small to cope with the growing number of larger boats and by the late nineteenth century fishing had become concentrated on the largest ports, such as Macduff and Fraserburgh, which had railway services. Hopes that Sandhaven would grow into a town never came to pass and instead it has remained a small village with a little used harbour.

New Aberdour is one of a dozen planned villages in Buchan that were founded in the late eighteenth and early nineteenth century by progressive landowners keen to improve the agricultural potential of their estates. The village was advertised in the *Aberdeen Journal* on several occasions in autumn 1797 and the first feus were purchased by tradesmen and labourers attracted by the opportunity to build their homes and acquire lots of land on which to grow crops and keep livestock. There were few public buildings in the village to begin with. The coaching inn was first, although twenty years passed before a church was built to replace the old kirk which lay about a mile away. Shops, the school and the parish hall were added in the Victorian period. New Aberdour remained a tradesman/crofter community throughout the nineteenth century; its population fell away after the 1870s largely as a result of slackening employment in agriculture. By the 1980s it was just over 300 and while growing car ownership opened up new job opportunities in nearby towns, this also led to the closure of local shops and services. Most recently the loss of the primary school can be explained by an aging population and fewer children.

Many of the photographs of the rural areas also capture facilities that once served small communities such as the shop and post office at Tyrie. The remaining rural schools have become more widely spaced and even churches have not been immune to this process, for example the Church of Scotland at Peathill on the outskirts of Rosehearty awaits a new use.

In spite of these changes, Buchan remains a very attractive area to live and work. Surveys have shown that local people have a very high quality of life, expressed in good health, employment, sports facilities and community life. Although many people now travel relatively long distances to work, for those who live here there remains a strong attachment to the places featured in this book.

The photographs have been arranged into a journey that begins in New Aberdour and then visits the nearby coast. Next, we head inland through the districts of Boyndlie, Tyrie and Peathill before exploring Rosehearty, Pitullie and Sandhaven.

This photograph covers the same ground as those on pages 7 and 9 but shows the opposite direction. Nothing seems to disturb the peace and quiet in the High Street of New Aberdour on a summer afternoon in 1970. Visit today and you would be pleasantly surprised to find that the scene has changed remarkably little apart from more parked vehicles and new street lighting. The convenience store on the west side of the street is still open, though it is the last one remaining here.

NEW ABERDOUR.

The first mention of New Aberdour occurs in an advertisement placed in the *Aberdeen Journal* of 26 September 1797. It announces that: 'WILLIAM GORDON Esq. of Aberdour intends to feu a certain extent of ground, in order to establish a VILLAGE upon his estate, near the Kirk of Aberdour, and invites industrious tradesmen and labourers to the place, where encouragement will be given.' Those interested were invited to a meeting at Ardlawhill a short distance away on 25 October when feus would be given off. The estate records show that William Gordon was present to explain the conditions of feuing and twenty-seven feus were sold that day. The growth of the village was modest, reaching a peak population of 642 at the 1881 Census. This view is from south of the village close to the road from Boyndlie and Strichen and looking towards High Street.

This photograph was taken from north-east of Elphin Street looking south-west, almost in the opposite direction to that of the previous picture. On the right can be seen the church, parish hall and the rear of the school. In general, photographs showing agricultural activity in the immediate vicinity of villages are quite rare, however there is evidence of a byre and sheds at the rear of the property on the left, a view of a lane that provided access to the fields, and in the top left the distinctive long rectangular fields known as lotted lands on the east side of the High Street. Crops such as oats, hay and turnips were grown, enabling villagers to keep a cow, and each year an auctioneer held a roup of growing crops on the village lands in August or September.

This view from around 1912 is of the southern section of High Street where many of the houses had been rebuilt within the last fifty years or so. The general merchant's shop at No. 18 (on the right of the photograph) was run by members of the Chalmers family for almost seventy years. George Chalmers (*c.* 1787–1852) began the business and his son George (1830–91) and wife Elspet followed, adding a post office, savings bank and bakery. George had been postmaster for thirty-six years when he died in 1891. An obituary in the *Banffshire Journal* on 24 February 1891 described him as 'a universal favourite' with all the personal qualities to manage a successful business. His sons William and George succeeded him but in 1919 the shop was sold to Alexander Cruden, a merchant from Garmond in Monquhitter Parish who continued the business until his death in 1938. The shop ceased trading in the early 1970s.

COMMERCIAL HOTEL, NEW ABERDOUR

The Commercial Hotel is about halfway up the High Street. It was the original village inn dating from 1798 and is now a listed building. This is where many of the community's social events were held, such as the dinners of the agricultural society. Advertisements in the 1920s described it as first class, admirably situated and close to 'the finest rock scenery in existence'. Fifty years later, not much seems to have changed and an article in the *Press and Journal* 'Weekend Review' of 26 July 1975 described the hotel as a 'valued local institution serving sound meals at a modest tariff'. After a succession of owners it was renamed the Dower Hotel in the late 1990s. In a full page feature in the *Fraserburgh Herald* in October 2004, yet another proprietor promised a new era for the hotel but this initiative seems to have been unsuccessful and today it is closed and has a forlorn appearance.

HIGH STREET, NEW ABERDOUR.

An early 1960s view of the northern half of High Street, looking towards the Church of Scotland at the junction with Elphin Street. There are few parked cars to interrupt the view of cottages with dormer windows that are typical in planned villages in Buchan. The sale of petrol at the Commercial Hotel is a reminder that many services and shops existed in villages at this time. In the late 1960s there were two general stores, a butcher's shop, a bank and a garage. Today, only one shop on the west side of the High Street remains open.

The origins of full-time policing in New Aberdour can be traced back to a meeting of local people in December 1876. This met with a speedy response from the authorities and in June the following year Constable G. Fyvie was stationed there. During the next twenty years constables were accommodated in rented properties, however in 1899 plans were finally approved for a police station in High Street costing £202. 18/6. Set slightly back from the line of the first generation of houses, it served the community until closure in 1966. The last constable was Louis Murray, who later served at Ballater and Braemar and was a founder member and subsequently Team Leader of Braemar Mountain Rescue. The former police station was sold in 1967 and is now a private house known as 'Inchbrakie'. The railings and gate have been removed, probably during the wartime scrap metal drive, the gap in the wall has been filled in so that the garden is now entered from the left and bushes have been planted at the front. Otherwise, externally the house itself has hardly changed since this photograph was taken.

Photographs of village lanes taken in summer 1970 may seem a surprising choice. However, the landscape in the lanes has changed much more over the last forty years than the High Street. When New Aberdour was founded there were back lanes on either side of the High Street which were linked by fifteen cross lanes. The back lanes ran behind the building plots and beyond these were the lotted lands or village fields. Small byres and sheds were often built beside the cross lanes. Part-time farming had only recently come to an end in most villages in Buchan in 1970 and byres such as the one in the left photograph were still very much in evidence. In the last forty years many of the rear gardens have been redeveloped with hard standings for vehicles, large garages and sheds, while the lanes now show signs of wear and tear caused by motor vehicles. On the east side of the village development has spilled over into the former lotted lands with several new houses built along Gordon Lane.

The Church of Scotland was built in 1818 to a design by John Smith of Aberdeen and can accommodate 800 people. Located at the head of the High Street, it has become the centrepiece of the village. On the south wall of the church is a small sundial and a tablet inscribed, 'The Church was erected by John Dingwall Esq. of Brucklay Patron and Principal Heritor of the Parish and Charles Forbes Esq., Proprietor of Auchmedden, MDCCCXVIII' (1818). It replaced the old church which lies on the road to Aberdour Shore (back cover). Like those in Rosehearty (page 29), the fountain and watering troughs commemorate Queen Victoria's Diamond Jubilee. The horse troughs are also a reminder that the village was situated at the junction of several country roads. *The 'Contour' Road Book of Scotland* (1896) describes the New Aberdour to Banff road as a 'fair road to Aberdour; thereafter it is a fearful and almost precipitous road till within a few miles of Macduff when it improves and is of a good surface.' The author remembers it as a severe test for his 1962 Austin Mini on visits to the area in the late 1960s and it is still a roller coaster ride even though many of the bends have been greatly improved.

Unlike other planned villages in Buchan, New Aberdour lacked a central square and an open space at the north end of High Street was used for the local fairs. The bellcote was originally part of the old parish church while the porch on the west wall of the church was added in 1885. The parish hall behind the church was built in 1892 and five years later a bazaar was held to clear off the remaining £300 of the debt incurred by the building costs. It was opened, not surprisingly, by local estate factor Charles Barclay of Aberdour House. The *Fraserburgh Advertiser* reported on 6 August that 'A small army of ladies did a brisk trade in raffling' and needless to say the event was a great success. The clock tower was added later and was the gift of Alexander Lovie, a farmer from Nether Boyndlie. In a short speech at the tower's official opening in January 1911, the laird, Alexander Dingwall Fordyce, reminded everyone that there was now no excuse for being late for school, for the ministers exceeding the time limit for their sermons, or for missing trains when the railway came to Aberdour (which sadly did not happen). The hall has served the community well over the years with activities such as concerts, dances and amateur dramatics taking place there, as well as badminton and church social events.

SCHOOL STREET, NEW ABERDOUR.

The school in the photograph dates from mid-Victorian times and educated children in the village and its rural hinterland until 1968. In 1906, the school log book reported 162 pupils attending. Like many rural schools, attendance was disrupted by severe weather in winter and at harvest time, such as in October 1917 when the steam threshing mill was in the village, 'the attendance [was] … only a little over 50% in the Senior room'. In the 1960s Aberdour School lost its secondary pupils and staff who were transferred to Rosehearty. In the mid 1960s additional land was acquired to build a new school at a cost of around £53,000 and this was officially opened on 18 October 1968 by Patrick Wolrige Gordon, MP for Aberdeenshire East. The *Education Committee Progress Report* (1967–1969) praised the open-plan teaching areas and the latest fittings and, to complete the modern image, the old school was demolished to make way for a car park. By 2009 the school roll had fallen to just seven compared with a peak of sixty-four in 1993. The 'new' school closed after a final day of celebrations that were reported in the *Fraserburgh Herald* on 9 July 2009. Local children now attend Rosehearty School.

Ploughmen were among the most respected and best paid farm servants because of their importance to the farm, their skills and long working hours spent at work in the fields as well as feeding and grooming their horses. Like other farm workers they were hired for six month periods and young men such as the one in the photograph would live in a chaumer, a small room at the end of the steading or above the stables. Showpiece photographs are quite common and were often taken on the day of a ploughing competition or an agricultural show. The horseman in the photograph, which was probably taken at Aberdour House farm, may have been successful at the annual Aberdour Agricultural Show which attracted competitors from half a dozen parishes.

Travelling a short distance west from the village there is a junction where the right turning heads downhill towards the Mill Farm, the manse and old church and eventually reaches the coast at what was known as Aberdour Shore. The farm and meal mill are mentioned in the Poll Tax returns of 1696 while Walter Macfarlane's *Geographical Collections* written in the 1720s states that 'the church is one of the oldest in the North of Scotland ... and stands hard by the seaside upon the Eastside of the Burn of Aberdour.' The prominent house in the centre of the photograph is the manse built in 1822/23. It remained in Church of Scotland ownership until 1955 and a few years later, as growing car ownership made such out of the way places more accessible, it became the Beach House Hotel. The hotel closed around 1989 and is now a private house. The churchyard and the remains of the old church are next door and an old dovecot is a feature of the boundary wall. They are well worth exploring. A stone dated 1593 is in memory of George Baird of Auchmedden, the mathematician, while another commemorates William Gordon, founder of the village who died in 1839 aged 67, as well as members of his family.

In this view, taken in a south-easterly direction from Bankhead Farm, the Corn Mill, cottages and the Mill Farm are all visible in the foreground while the old kirk and manse are in the distance. In the churchyard, there is a stone that commemorates the life of Samuel Craik, tenant of Mill Farm, 'who having for the space of 53 years discharged the office of Schoolmaster in this parish died 7 July 1820 aged 70.' He was also an auctioneer and was factor to William Gordon, laird of Aberdour.

Seen here between the cliffs in the foreground, the Barn Door is a rock just off the coast west of Aberdour Bay and close to Strahangles Point. The red sandstone rocks have been sculpted into inlets and sea caves that add interest to this spectacular stretch of coastline. Francis Douglas who visited in 1782 on a tour of the east coast was in awe of the wild seascapes here. He wrote that 'The highest rocks are between Auchmedden and Aberdour. As you approach their summit, if the sea be rough, the roaring of the waves below, and the wild screaming of the fowls above, form a hideous concert.'

Standing at the entrance to 'Jock's Cave' is Edward Reid, known as Jock. He was born in Ireland in the early 1840s and was recorded as living in the cave by the 1911 census. He came into Rosehearty to do his shopping and sold hand-made brushes. Local people knew little about him and some even thought that he might have been a German spy. His last days were spent at the Buchan Combination Poorhouse in Maud where he died in 1918. Reid's death certificate records his usual address as: 'At cave sea shore, Aberdour'.

Boyndlie lies at the crossroads of the Banff to Fraserburgh former turnpike road (A98) and the country road from Strichen to New Aberdour about 1.5 miles west of Tyrie. In the foreground of this view is Boyndlie Post Office and shop, built by Boyndlie estate on land known as the School Croft. It can be traced back to 1880 when it was run by James Morrice who previously had a shop in New Aberdour. In 1910 the tenancy was taken up by William Farquhar from New Deer and it continued to operate as a post office, shop, petrol retailer and carpenter's business in family ownership after his death in 1947. The building on the extreme left of the picture partly hidden by trees is the Episcopal School which dates from 1864. At the beginning of the twentieth century the school roll at Boyndlie was 103, however numbers steadily fell with just 33 pupils attending in 1945. The final entry in the school log book on 30 June 1961 was as follows: 'Duties at Boyndlie School terminate today. School is being temporarily closed pending notification of official closing. 10 Scholars are being transferred to Tyrie School and 1 to Strichen.' The building was vacant throughout the 1960s and is now a private house.

When the *New Statistical Account* was published in 1845 the only post office in Tyrie Parish was in the village of New Pitsligo. However, the 1851 census records John Joss, who was just twenty years old, 'merchant grocer & clothier' at Nether Boyndlie (Ardequharn) on the main Fraserburgh to Banff road. Ten years later *Slater's Directory* lists a post office here with Joss in charge and it also appears on the first Ordnance Survey maps of the parish from 1870. A century later it was in the same location and it continued to offer postal services until November 2003 when Rosemary Laird, the long-serving postmistress retired. The house and its distinctive porch can still be found on the left hand side of the A98 when heading towards Fraserburgh.

The history of rural schools can be fascinating and Tyrie is no exception. The school house was located close to Tyrie Parish Church on the east side of the Banff to Fraserburgh road. Records begin in 1873, a year after Alexander Copland, who was born in Strichen and had teaching experience in Edinburgh and Fraserburgh, became head teacher. He served Tyrie for more than thirty years before retiring in August 1905 and afterwards he moved to Edinburgh where he died in 1921 aged 80. This photograph is almost certainly that of Alexander Copland along with his daughter and housekeeper, Elizabeth Lena, who was 23 years old at the 1901 census. Today, Tyrie School is still open, occupying a building nearby which was built in the early 1930s.

Boyndlie House, the seat of the Ogilvie-Forbes family, was built in 1814 on the site of a seventeenth century house. Alexander Smith in his *New History of Aberdeenshire*, published in 1875, described it as 'a substantial modern building without architectural pretensions – picturesquely situated, and surrounded with trees, some of which are very old. The garden has a southern exposure, and is well protected on all sides.'

Peathill is a small hamlet close to the old and new Pitsligo parish churches. Near a minor road junction, where the left fork leads to Sandhaven and the right towards the A98 at Mid Ardlaw, there are several houses and the short terrace of cottages in the photograph. At the beginning of the twentieth century the small shop was a merchant's premises and in 1904 it passed to William Burnett Rennie, a tailor. In the early 1920s Rennie became a market gardener, a business which he continued with his son until his death in 1943. The small building between the shop and the cottages is a storage hut and, partly rebuilt, it is still in use today. The cottages have changed little since this photograph was taken but any trace of the shop has long vanished.

The first kirk at Peathill was built in the early 1630s just before the Parish of Pitsligo separated from Aberdour. In 1890 growing population and an aging church building seemed good reasons to think that a new church should be built (it can be seen on the right of this photograph). Its funding, however, provoked huge controversy and its opening was certainly a muted affair. The *East Aberdeenshire Observer* on 30 October 1890 reported 'there was no special ceremony … The services were directed to harvest thanksgiving and a preparation for the half-yearly sacrament.' All property owners in the parish were levied 6 shillings in the pound of feu duty to pay for the parish church. However, members of the Free Church who had paid for the building of their own church only a few years earlier refused to pay the levy and the visit of the sheriff officer to serve summonses on the defaulters led to a riot. Police reinforcements were called from Fraserburgh, arrests were made and four fishermen were found guilty of offences of rioting and obstructing the police. The minister, Walter Gregor, who had intended retiring in Rosehearty, instead left the town and moved to Bonnyrigg in Midlothian where he died in 1897. The new church remained in use until 21 September 1997 when the last service was held. Ironically, since then Church of Scotland services have been held in the former United Free Church building and the adjacent manse is now the home of the minister as well.

PITSLIGO CASTLE, ROSEHEARTY.

The ruins of Pitsligo Castle, south of Rosehearty, are as impressive as this photograph suggests. The writer of the *New Statistical Account* described 'walls 6–7 feet thick, probably reared three centuries ago.' Further building took place around 1570, but it was looted and destroyed by Flemish troops stationed there after the 1745 rebellion. The castle is flanked by a walled enclosure to the west and a walled garden to the north, which in early Victorian times was greatly admired for the fruit it produced. It is owned by Pitsligo Castle Trust which has plans to restore the gardens to their former glory and has carried out remedial work on the stone structures.

Egypt is the name of a farm located just off the coast road between Aberdour and Rosehearty. At the roadside the distinctive camel sign must cause passing motorists to ponder on its name, which dates from the eighteenth century when biblical names were popular. A track on the farm's land leads to an inlet called Quarry Haven where a salmon fishermen's bothy, icehouses and a jetty were built in the mid-nineteenth century and became known as the Egypt salmon fishing station. Salmon fishers were recorded here at the 1851 and 1861 censuses. After the First World War, the sea fishings in Aberdour were bought by David Powrie, originally from Perthshire and a major force in salmon fishing. He also leased the adjacent sea fishings at Auchmedden and Rosehearty. The Powrie family was connected with the area until the Second World War after which a succession of local fishermen-tacksmen owned the Aberdour sea fishings. Stake nets used to catch the fish during the fishing season (February to August) and a fishing coble needed to haul and remove the nets from the sea can be seen in the photograph. The growth of fish farming, the drop in fish prices as a result, and leasing of sea fishings by river salmon fishery boards to conserve fish stocks have all contributed to ending stake net fishing on the coast in Aberdour and Rosehearty.

The arrival of the bus outside the post office seems to have been a major event. Motor bus services between New Aberdour, Rosehearty and Fraserburgh began in June 1906 when Charles Gordon advertised in the *Buchan Observer* that he was starting a service between Fraserburgh and New Aberdour. Later the route was operated by William Simpson, tenant of the Temperance Hotel. In 1912 the Great North of Scotland Railway Company took over the service and Simpson became a conductor. The photograph is probably of one of the first services run by the railway company. The *Fraserburgh Advertiser* on 22 November reported that 'The vehicles are large and roomy … All the other vehicles run for the convenience of passengers are off the road ...' The Railway-operated bus services continued until 1927 and shortly afterwards services were begun by Simpson's Motors whose buses plied the route until the mid 1960s when Walter Alexander & Sons (Northern) purchased the business. The tall figure standing in the middle of the square is Constable William Smith who served at Rosehearty between 1911 and 1913 and retired as an inspector at Fraserburgh in 1929. He can also be seen outside the Masonic Temple (page 33).

The Diamond Jubilee Fountain in the Square is inscribed on the side facing the camera 'Victoria Regina 1837 Sixty Years 1897'. About 10 feet high, it was designed by Victor Mitchell, architect of Aberdeen who was born in Rosehearty. The crown is made of Peterhead granite and the drinking bowls are made of polished granite from Rubislaw quarry. Above the inscription is the burgh coat of arms and on the opposite side is the Dingwall Fordyce family coat of arms, a hart. A horse trough is on the far side of the fountain just out of view. The fountain was officially opened by the daughters of the estate factor, Charles Barclay of Aberdour House, on 22 June 1897.

In an age before mass car ownership, four local men are waiting at the bus stop in an otherwise deserted Rosehearty Square. The bus is in the livery of James Sutherland, Peterhead, who had the licence to run the service to Aberdeen via Fraserburgh. Sutherland (1862–1933) was a very enterprising and successful businessman. He was born in Buchanhaven and began work when a boy, transporting fishermen's nets with a pony and cart. Sutherland became involved in horse hiring and contracting and as the business grew he bought a former curing yard in St Peter Street, Peterhead, which became known as the Victoria Stables. His business developed into one of the largest independent road transport companies in Scotland, giving work to 130 people. In the early 1930s Sutherland buses operated on most major routes in Aberdeenshire and the fleet was the largest in the North East when the business was nationalised in 1950, after which their network passed to Walter Alexander & Sons.

Five shops including the post office are located in the Square but there are few shoppers to be seen while an Aberdeen-bound double decker in James Sutherland livery waits at the terminus. The photograph is helpful in locating other views of Rosehearty. The post office at No. 10 the Square is on the left (later the Bay Hotel, recently renamed Davron Hotel); the Masonic Temple is tucked almost out of sight in the far left-hand corner of the Square; the Forbes Arms Hotel is next to the tree on the left of the street leading into the distance (Pitsligo Street); John Gibb's shop was in the last group of buildings in Pitsligo Street and the fountain in the centre of the Square commemorates Queen Victoria's Diamond Jubilee, celebrated in Rosehearty on 22 June 1897.

A bus operated by Simpson's Motors of Rosehearty, seen here waiting for passengers to board at Mealmarket Street Bus Station in Aberdeen. The bus was first registered in 1952 to Rhondda Transport Company, a major bus operator in South Wales, and along with several others it was purchased by Simpson's in 1964. The business dates from around 1930 and was managed by James Shearer Simpson (1898–1955), son of William Simpson who ran the Temperance Hotel. When it was taken over by Walter Alexander & Sons (Northern) in 1966, the company owned thirty-one buses including LNY 358. Since then family members have run a taxi business and have set up Simpson's Coaches which are still in business in Rosehearty as a coach hire and tour company.

Below: The Forbes Lodge of Rosehearty was probably founded in 1743 as there were anniversary celebrations recorded fifty years later. In 1911 the lodge paid £50 for a site on the south-east corner of the Square; funds were raised by holding a bazaar and the masonic temple was built in the following year. The temple remains little changed externally, though the fine railings have disappeared. The lodge continues to hold the traditional Masons' Walk, one of only two such events in Scotland. Newspaper reports during the late nineteenth century show that the walk took place on Auld Yule (originally 5 January in the Julian calendar). This was followed by the annual election of office bearers and a dinner in the Forbes Arms. A ball held in the Fordyce Street Hall concluded what was known as Rosehearty Field Day. Today the Masons' Walk is held on 2 January when it passes through every street in the town. Around 150 masons take part, watched by a large crowd of onlookers and the event remains an important social occasion.

Above: In 1974 the post office was at No. 7 Pitsligo Street, but just like the one in New Aberdour it has moved a number of times over the years. At the beginning of the twentieth century the post office was on the south-east side of the Square (pages 30 and 31) but in January 1960 Jane Reid purchased No. 7 Pitsligo Street and later that year the ground floor was converted for use as a post office. She was still there when this photograph was taken in 1974, however the following year it was sold to Alexander and Isobel Downie. In the late 1990s the post office returned to the Square but closed due to poor revenues. Services were eventually reinstated in the butcher's shop in Ward Road in June 2009.

59392. FORRES ARMS HOTEL, ROSEHEARTY.

The Forbes Arms Hotel in Pitsligo Street has changed out of all recognition since this photograph was taken in the early 1960s. The tree, petrol pumps and entrance have all disappeared and most of the frontage has been obscured by the construction of a new entrance area and a long, flat-roofed building in a style typical of what was in vogue in the late 1960s. This building housed 'Jasmyn's Niteclub', a very popular venue, where dinner dances were held and live bands, discos and karaoke entertained the locals. In the 1920s advertisements in *Macdonald's Scottish Directory and Gazetteer* described it as 'nicely situated in the centre of the town; gentlemen, tourists and others, will find every home comfort combined with moderate charges.' In the sixty years before the photograph was taken the hotel was managed by members of only three families, the Hendersons (1898–1939), the Bannermans from Fraserburgh (1939–1956) and, afterwards, the Simpsons who still own it. In 1902 William Henderson was first to advertise a bus service from the hotel connecting with trains arriving at Fraserburgh Station.

Pitsligo Street is the main street in the older part of the town. It also forms the road towards the church and Aberdour. On the left is the shop owned by John Gibb, draper and general merchant. Gibb was born in 1835 at the Howe of Byth in King Edward Parish and although apprenticed to the long-established merchant's business of William Tennant in Cuminestown, he became a school teacher in Fraserburgh before moving to Rosehearty in the mid 1860s where he ran the shop in Pitsligo Street for more than thirty-five years. He was appointed provost in 1896 and served until his death in 1910. There have been many changes since this photograph was taken. A lock-up garage has replaced the shop and the middle house on the left has been built-up to two stories. Many of the houses on the right hand side were replaced by local authority housing in the inter-war period and only the house in the distance at right angles to the street remains, although it is now used as a store.

The west end of Pitsligo Street, where only a few buildings remain before the open countryside. On the right is the police station, which was built in 1864 and closed on 1 February 1993, the school, and beyond is the United Presbyterian Church which was completed in 1882, a year after the ordination of the Rev. William Paton Ogilvie at a time when the congregation was growing steadily. Built at a cost of £1,550, it was able to accommodate about 400 people. It replaced an older church near the harbour in Union Street which is now a private house. After the merger of the Free Church and the United Presbyterian Church in 1900, it became known as the United Free Church of Rosehearty. The Rev. Ogilvie died in 1906 after contracting pneumonia while attending a Sunday school picnic. The tragedy affected the whole community and as a result the congregation that attended Loch Street Church merged with that of Pitsligo Street. In 1929, the United Free Church amalgamated with the Church of Scotland, whose parish church, known as the Hill Church was at Peathill, 1½ miles south of the town. With the closure of the Hill Church in 1997, the only functioning church in Rosehearty is the one in Pitsligo Street. The manse, which was built in 1896, is next to the church.

Rosehearty School is situated on the west side of Pitsligo Street. The school building, which dates from mid-Victorian times, was closed in 2005 and, although there were calls for it to be preserved, it was subsequently demolished to make way for the entrance and car park of the new school. The school had been extended in 1959, however in 1984 the secondary classes at Rosehearty were transferred to Fraserburgh and by the early 2000s the extension was in poor physical condition. In October 2005 a large new primary school incorporating a nursery class and community library was completed at a cost of £4.5 million.

Tennis courts and a bowling green were built on the outskirts of Rosehearty shortly after the end of the First World War. Plans were approved by the town council in November 1920 and opened two years later. The tennis courts closed due to lack of use around 1960 and the site is now a car park for the bowling club which continues to thrive. Beyond and partly hidden by trees is the former Free Church manse which was purchased by George Forbes, a local boat builder, in 1920. In the early 1960s it became the Cliff View Hotel, owned by his daughter Jean (Jeannie Simpson) and later by her son. 'Sea Views and Sea Food' figured in newspaper advertisements for the hotel in its heydays. The hotel was sold about ten years ago after the owners retired and it is now a private house again.

CLEARING WRECK, WEST ROCKS, ROSEHEARTY

Shipwrecks were a common occurrence on the north coast of Buchan. Several in the vicinity of Rosehearty have been the occasions for heroism and tragedy, although the wreck in the picture has a very different story. The ship, broken into two sections by the impact on the rocks, was the German First World War destroyer G 103 which had been scuttled at Scapa Flow in 1919. It was raised in September 1925 and as it was being towed to the ship breakers at Rosyth in the early hours of Wednesday 25 November the tow ropes to the tug snapped in a gale some 20 miles north of Rattray Head. It was driven onto the rocks at Lochielair, one mile west of Rosehearty, and photographs showing the destroyer broken into two sections appeared in the *Aberdeen Press and Journal* two days later.

NORTH STREET, OLD SEATOWN, ROSEHEARTY

The Seatown, north-west of the old harbour, consists of two rows of single-storey cottages with their gable ends facing towards the sea. This is the oldest area of housing in Rosehearty and dates from the seventeenth century. The Seatown, like Pitullie (pages 54 and 55), has always been a fishing community. The enumerators' books of the 1901 census show that virtually every head of household was a fisherman or was in fishing-related employment.

The Old Harbour, Rosehearty

Low tide in the west harbour with a mix of small inshore craft and two larger herring drifters. FR270 'Daisy II', closest to the camera, was built in 1908 for a group of fishermen from Cairnbulg near Fraserburgh. Although there are a number of men and boys in the photograph there appears to be very little fishing activity. Compared with today where groups of lobster pots and plastic fish boxes line the quay, little of the hardware associated with part-time fishing is in view.

THE HARBOUR, ROSEHEARTY

After the herring boom had collapsed and until the Second World War most local men worked as fishermen, although they operated out of Fraserburgh. Those boats which continued to be based at the harbour were involved in fishing for white fish. Gradually, fishing at Rosehearty became a part-time activity and by the 1950s there were only around fifteen small boats still based there such as those derived from the 'baldie' design which had their masts well forward.

THE SWIMMING POOL, ROSEHEARTY   59495

The construction of open air seawater swimming pools or lidos was fashionable in the inter-war period when outdoor sporting activities attracted a large following. The pool in a corner of the harbour at Rosehearty was the last seawater pool to be built in Scotland and was not opened until 1959. Maitland Mackie, dairy farmer and convener of the County Education Committee, presided at the official opening and the pool appears to have been an instant success with almost 10,000 paid admissions in the first month. Unfortunately the golden years did not last long and fifteen years later a report in the *Press and Journal* on 13 August 1974 noted that although the season was from early June to the end of August the pool had only been open a total of 10 days and 'yesterday lay empty and locked up due to lack of staff'. Following local government reorganization, Banff and Buchan District Council were supportive at first, however early in 1989 it was decided not to spend an estimated £20,000 on repairs to prevent leaking and so the pool closed. It was demolished a few years later and the corner of the harbour became a small beach again.

Damaged Pier, 14th March, 1906, Rosehearty

The local newspapers all reported on the damage caused by a particularly severe gale that began on the night of Sunday 11 March 1906 and continued throughout the following day. The *Buchan Observer* noted that 'no such storm of wind and snow has been experienced during the whole of the winter'. Damage in Rosehearty was extensive and around 30 feet of the parapet of the pier sheltering Port Rae was demolished – as shown in this photograph – and part of the esplanade near the Temperance Hotel (page 51) was washed away. More recently, the Community Council has become increasingly concerned about storm damage to Port Rae which in addition to being a familiar part of the coastal landscape, provides shelter for small pleasure craft and is a bulwark against coastal erosion.

Loch Street is part of the grid of streets north-west of the Square known as the New Town. The fisherman in the foreground is drying 'snoods' that would carry hooks most commonly baited with mussels that were collected from the shore and these would be attached to the main line. At the far end of the street is the Free Church which was built by 1845 shortly after the 'Disruption' within the Church of Scotland. It cost a modest £129 to build using red sandstone and was known as 'The Reid Kirkie', with most of its membership drawn from the Seatown. In 1906 the congregation joined with the United Free Church in Pitsligo Street and after a time the latter church became their sole place of worship. Loch Street church was sold to the town council in 1920, becoming offices and a fisherman's store. It is now a boat builder's workshop.

MID STREET ROSEHEARTY.

Mid Street along with Kirk Street, Loch Street, Fordyce Street, Dingwall Street and Well Street make up the nineteenth-century New Town area which was built on the Fisherland, the former crofts of the fishermen in the Seatown. This area has wide streets and substantial cottages, many with dormer windows. In 1825 only a few houses had been built on Loch Street and by 1867 plots had been laid out throughout much of the area. As a result Rosehearty was for a time one of the fastest growing coastal towns in the North East and many of the houses were built by fishermen during the boom years in the industry. The spacious layout is in contrast with the older tightly-packed properties in the Seatown.

Dingwall Street, Rosehearty

Dingwall Street was the last street to be built in the New Town area. It is not shown on the first Ordnance Survey map (1871) and ten years later the census recorded only seven families living there. Many of the houses in the photograph, which is postmarked 1917, were only twenty or thirty years old by that time. The scene today is remarkably similar to 100 years ago.

A2997 ROSEHEARTY, ABERDEENSHIRE

This view taken from the west pier, near the entrance to the old harbour, demonstrates the haphazard development that has taken place along Shore Street and Union Street towards Port Rae. The oldest buildings, including a house dating from 1811, are close to the harbour while the caravan site and several council houses are in the middle distance. On the horizon can be seen Pitsligo Parish Church, built in 1892, while at a slightly lower level are the ruins of Pitsligo Castle.

Viewed from the end of the breakwater is a 'ripper' that was used extensively for small line fishing in inshore fishing grounds. It was common practice for fishermen to row these small craft from the harbour. They were very vulnerable in bad weather, but the two boys dangling their feet in the water and the presence of a well-dressed girl suggests that this was probably a pleasure trip on a fine day. The landmarks from right to left are the net factory, Temperance Hotel and lastly the Mason's Arms on the eastern edge of town.

Union Street. Rosehearty.

This view is taken from the eastern fringe of the town with the links immediately behind the photographer. This area is part of the Old Town which focuses on the Square and was developed after Rosehearty became a burgh of barony in the late seventeenth century. On the left is the long-established Mason's Arms Hotel while the Temperance Hotel seen in more detail on the next page is the two-storey building on the right of the photograph. With the exception of some redevelopment about halfway along the street, this scene has changed relatively little over the course of the last century.

The Temperance Movement was popular in the nineteenth century and coffee houses and hotels where no alcohol was served were opened. The Temperance Hotel in Link Street (later Union Street), overlooking the links, was opened by Samuel Hadden, a horse hirer who rented the premises between 1895 and 1898 before leaving for South Queensferry to manage another Temperance hotel. In Rosehearty, the tenancy passed to William Simpson, horse hirer and bus owner. The hotel was a favourite with Rosehearty golfers whose course on the links was nearby. It was also popular with summer visitors and people came from as far as Glasgow to stay. During the peak summer season, when every room in the hotel was fully booked, the hotelier's family would sleep in the bell-shaped tents on the lawn. In 1931, the lease was taken up by James Davidson Taylor, who married one of Simpson's daughters, Euphemia. The hotel closed in the early 1940s and later it was purchased by Frederick Barclay Simpson, one of William Simpson's sons, and once again it became a private house.

East, Rosehearty

The photograph of the eastern part of Rosehearty (above) covers the area from Link Street (later Union Street) passing the Temperance Hotel on the foreshore, the net factory and the buildings flanking the Square which are in the middle of the photograph. Vessels sheltering in the lee of the Port Rae breakwater (new harbour) are also visible. In the view to the west (opposite), the masts of a boat in the old harbour are visible and in the town buildings on Pitsligo Street are in the middle distance and new houses along one of the streets in the New Town are visible towards the left of the photograph. The street closest to the camera is Brucklay Street where houses were built in the late nineteenth century and in the foreground are small strips of agricultural land and several mounds of seaweed ready to be used as fertiliser. These and other lots of land were rented by about thirty tradesmen and labourers in the town while carters and dairymen also had lots. Local authority housing now occupies many of these fields. These were begun just before the Second World War (Queen Street) and after hostilities ended a start was made to Summers Road and Dundarg Road. The scheme was completed with the building of Queen's Crescent in the late 1960s.

Approaching Pitullie from Rosehearty, all the houses in this part of the village are gable end to the sea and typical of seatowns throughout the North East. They would have housed fishermen's families at the beginning of the twentieth century. Before Sandhaven harbour was built, the harbour at Pitullie was a narrow channel between rocks that gave access to the beach, where boats were pulled up above the high tide mark between seasons. Outwardly little changed, most of the houses have been extensively modernised and are now attractive to people commuting to work in Fraserburgh and further afield.

Closer to Sandhaven, this part of the Seatown has houses situated parallel to the main road in contrast to those at the far end of the street that are laid out at right-angles to it. Pitullie probably dates from the sixteenth century and at the end of the following century nine seamen were paying poll tax there. When the new harbour was being built it had a population of around 230. This changed little during the next fifty years and at the 1901 census it stood at 219.

THE HARBOUR, SANDHAVEN.

SDN. 5.

In 1835 the fishermen of Pitullie petitioned the Board of Fisheries for better harbour facilities. The site chosen was a short distance from the old seatown of Pitullie and feus in a new village called Sandhaven were advertised in the *Aberdeen Journal* on 7 November 1838. In 1869 the South Jetty, on the left of the photograph, was completed and a large new breakwater, part of which can be seen on the right of the photograph, was constructed between 1873 and 1885. At its peak about 100 boats fished from the harbour which also attracted coastal shipping. A boatbuilding business was established that only closed in 1991 and the boat yard is now used for decommissioning ships. The harbour, which had suffered from decades of neglect and damage by storms, has been purchased by the Sandhaven and Pitullie Harbour Trust and there are plans to bring it back to life by encouraging yachts and leisure craft to berth there.